compiled by

CHRONICLE BOOKS
SAN FRANCISCO

everything reverberates

THOUGHTS ON DESIGN

Printed in Hong Kong.

Library of Congress Cataloging-in-Publication Data:
Everything reverberates: thoughts on design/ compiled by Chronicle Books.
    p. cm.
    Includes bibliographical references.
    ISBN 0-8118-1934-5
    I. Chronicle Books (Firm)
PN6084.D46E95   1998   97-36634
082—dc21   CIP

Cover design: Macintosh computer and Pamela Geismar
Book design: Michelle Benzer, Michael Carabetta, Sarah Crumb,
Patricia Evangelista, Julia Flagg, Pamela Geismar, Carole Goodman,
Kristin Holder, Natalie Johnstone, Sing Lin, Laura Lovett, Sushma Patel,
Liz Rico, Toby Salk, Joseph Stitzlein, Martine Trélaün, Nina Turner.
Quote research: Sarah Crumb
Prepress lifesaving: Prepress Assembly

Distributed in Canada by Raincoast Books
8680 Cambie Street
Vancouver, B.C. V6P 6M9

10 9 8 7 6 5 4 3 2 1

Chronicle Books
85 Second Street
San Francisco, CA 94105

Web Site: www.chronbooks.com

A designer should use only these typefaces: 5

1 Bodoni
2 Helvetica
3 Times Roman
4 Century *and*
5 Futura. —Massimo Vignelli

" good desig

AT
LEAST
PART OF THE
TIME, INCLUDES
THE CRITERIA
OF BEING
DIRECT IN
RELATION TO
THE PROBLEM AT
HAND—NOT
OBSCURE,
TRENDY, OR
STYLISH. A NEW
LANGUAGE,
VISUAL OR
VERBAL, MUST
BE COUCHED IN
A LANGUAGE
THAT IS
ALREADY
UNDERSTOOD. "

ivan chermayeff

VISUALIZE

"

IN OUR TIME THERE ARE MANY ARTISTS WHO

go for
novelty,

AND SEE THEIR VALUE AND
JUSTIFICATION IN NOVELTY;
BUT THEY ARE WRONG.
NOVELTY IS HARDLY EVER
IMPORTANT. WHAT MATTERS IS
ALWAYS JUST THE ONE THING:
TO PENETRATE TO THE VERY
HEART OF A THING, AND
CREATE IT BETTER.

"

enri-marie-raymond de toulouse-lautrec

We live in
a culture
where
the one who
shouts the
loudest
gets the most
attention.

It's not in the
vulgar,
it's not in the
shock
that one finds
art.

And
it's not
in the
excessively
beautiful.

It's in
between;
it's in nuance.

Duane Michals

ve broken the blue boundary of color limits, come out into the white; Side me comrade-pilots swim in this infinity. I have established the haphore of Suprematism. I have beaten the lining of the colored sky, orn it away and in the sack that formed itself, I have put color and knotted it. Swim! The free white sea, infinity, lies before you.

— Kasimir Malevich

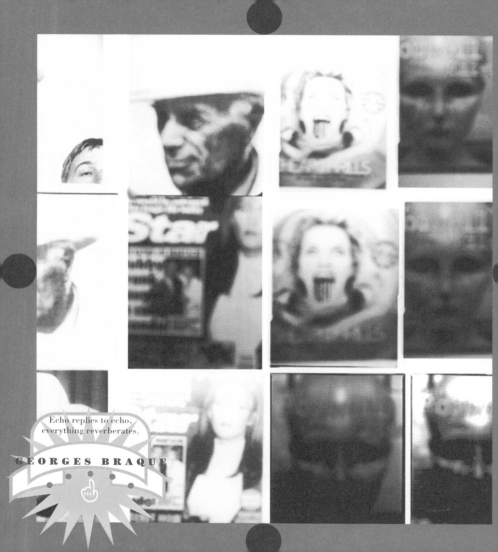

Echo replies to echo,
everything reverberates.

GEORGES BRAQUE

if you

manage to do something

following your instinct
as closely as possible,

then

you have succeeded;

but that's
truly
exceptional.

It   very

rarely

happens.

—*Francis Bacon*

It's a blue collar job.

It burns up ideas,

and you just have to
keep feeding it.

—FRED WOODWARD

DESIGN IS EASY.

All you do is stare
at the screen
until drops of blood
form on your forehead.

MARTY NEUMEIER

(TO PARAPHRASE GENE FOWLER)

Perfect communication is person-to-person. You see me, hear me, smell me, touch me. Television's the second form of communication; you can see me and hear me. Radio is the next; you hear me, but you don't see me. And then comes print. You can't see or hear me, so you must be able to interpret the kind of person I am from what is on the printed page. That's where typographic design comes in.

[AARON BURNS]

CAFFEINE FREE
The richest communication will be that which selects just the right combination of senses, allowing us to rely on our memories and imaginations. -Wendy Richmond

2 LITER 67.6 FL OZ (2 QT 3.6 FL OZ)

To create one's own world in any of the arts takes courage.

— Georgia O'Keeffe

Content comes first...yet excellent design can catch people's eyes and impress the contents on their memory. — Hideki Nakajima

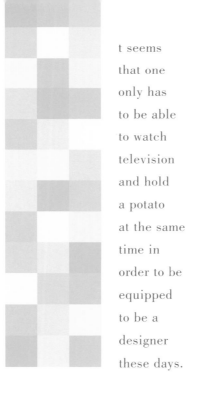

t seems
that one
only has
to be able
to watch
television
and hold
a potato
at the same
time in
order to be
equipped
to be a
designer
these days.

Glenn Martinez

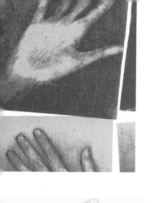
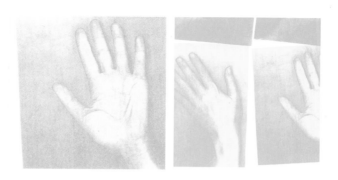

It is not easy to know what you like.
Most people fool themselves
their entire lives about this.
Self-acquaintance is a rare condition.
                                    - Robert Henri

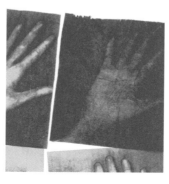

I make solutions that nobody wants to problems that don't exist.
—Alvin Lustig

(desigi

What distinguishes a designer sheep from a designer goat is the
ability to stroke a cliché until it purrs like a metaphor.
—Alan Fletcher

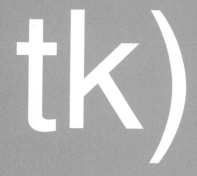

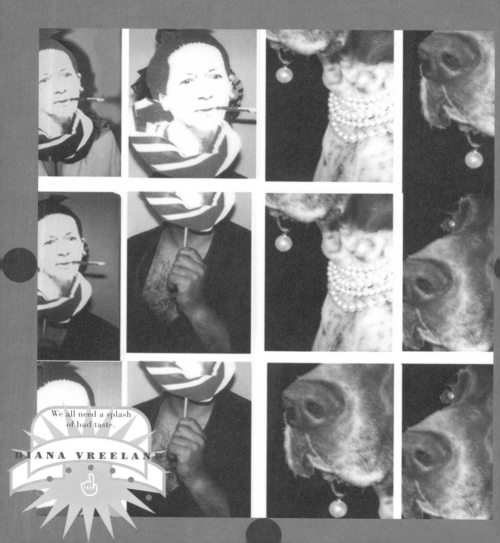

We all need a splash
of bad taste.

DIANA VREELAND

YOU HAVE TO BE INTERESTED
IN CULTURE TO DESIGN FOR IT.
-LORRAINE WILD

Sometimes
there is simply no need
to be either
clever or original.

— *Ivan Chermayeff*

agitate,
agitate,
agitate.
~ leslie sherr on philippe starck

IT IS ONLY WITH THE
HEART THAT ONE
CAN SEE RIGHTLY.
WHAT IS ESSENTIAL
IS INVISIBLE TO THE
EYE. ANTOINE DE
SAINT EXUPÉRY

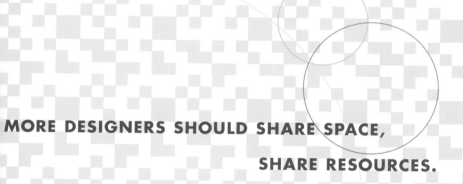

MORE DESIGNERS SHOULD SHARE SPACE,

SHARE RESOURCES.

SORT OF AN UPSCALE COMMUNISM.

april greiman

the word and image are one.

—hugo ba

The words graphic designer, architect, or industrial designer stick in my throat, giving me a sense of limitation, of specialization within the specialty, of a relationship to society and form itself that is unsatisfactory and incomplete. This inadequate set of terms to describe an active life reveals only partially the still undefined nature of the designer

AL-
VIN
Lustig

28

[Graphic design] is
the paradise of individuality,
eccentricity, heresy, abnormality,
hobbies, and humors.

~george santayana

What the creative act means is the unfolding of the human psyche in the sudden realization that one has taken a lot of disconnected pieces and *found*, not *done*, a way of putting them together.

—George Nelson

Design must seduce,
shape, and perhaps
more importantly,
evoke emotional response.

—APRIL GREIMAN

UGLINESS
DOES NOT SELL.

RAYMOND LOEWY

32

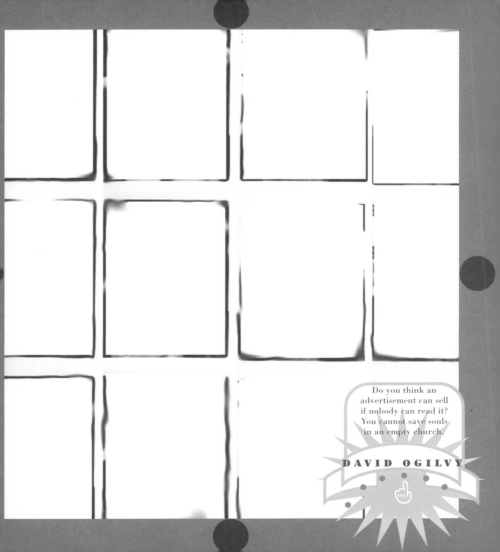

Do you think an
advertisement can sell
if nobody can read it?
You cannot save souls
in an empty church.

DAVID OGILVY

When it comes to handling text, **read** **ability**

I like to challenge the audience a bit,

but I know enough

to back off

when you really want people to read it.

—*MICHAEL MABRY*

Everybody in advertising
are happy, cars are nev
shiny, food looks like it
myself, "How stupid are
going one direction and a
pletely different direction
No design works unless it
common by the people for

—*Adrian Forty*

blonde, beautiful, families in traffic, everything is incredibly tasteful. I ask ? How come the world is rtising is going in a com-

—Oliviero Toscani

bodies ideas that are held om the object is intended.

symmetry is static—that is to say quiet—that is to say, inconspicuous

William Addison Dwiggins

ego

I think it's really important that we keep experimenting
all the time. But I think the worst thing is to become completely addicted
to something, even the computer.
GETTING ADDICTED TO
DESIGN IS BAD FOR DESIGN.
~ andy altmann

I don't believe any imagery should ever be given so much power that it cannot be played with.

—*James Jebbia*

YOU
READ
BEST
WHAT
YOU
READ
MOSL.

" I will do anything to support

individual means of

EXPRESSION

and if this means there are a million typefaces,

I'll support that, because I think people should

... be allowed to make their own. The ability

to design typefaces on the Macintosh is a true

REVOLUTION

....It means that design is no longer a kind

of temple. Everyone should be taught how

to communicate visually. **"**

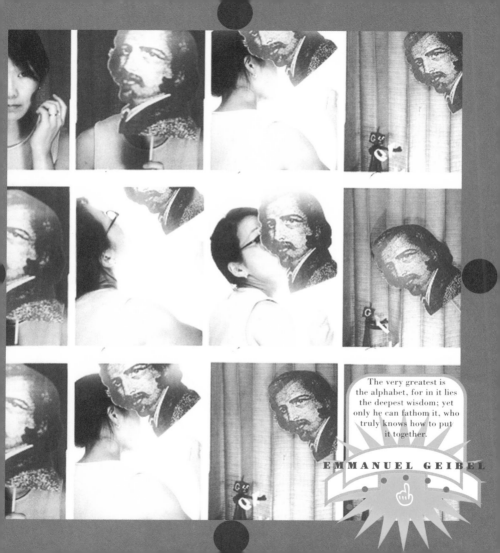

The very greatest is
the alphabet, for in it lies
the deepest wisdom; yet
only he can fathom it, who
truly knows how to put
it together.

EMMANUEL GEIBEL

My ads [for the film *The Man with the Golden Arm*] were so reductive, they became metaphors.

—Saul Bass

A FLOURISH

REQUIRES EXTRAORDINARY TASTE, BUT
IF IT IS SUCCESSFUL IF THE RIGHT
RELATIONSHIP IS FOUND, SUCH LETTERING
IS QUITE INCOMPARABLE, SO MUCH SO THAT

ONE COULD FALL IN LOVE WITH IT.

—FYODOR DOSTOYEVSKY

Without the aesthetic, design is either the humdrum repetition of familiar clichés or the wild scramble for novelty. Without the aesthetic, the computer is but a mindless speed machine, producing effects without substance, form without relevant content, or content without meaningful form.

— Paul Rand

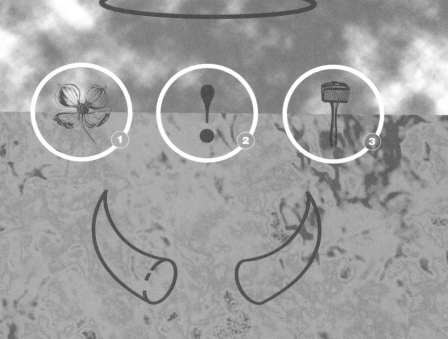

Design requires esthetics[1], inspiration[2], and guts[3]...
To me, nothing is more vibrant than having the power
to do something but not having the experience of

knowing what's right and what's wrong.

~ tibor kalman

I HAVE ALWAYS RAILED AGAINST IDEOLOGICAL PURITY,
OR ANY OTHER KIND. AT PUSH PIN WE FOUND

corruption was
more interesting
than purity.

~ milton glaser

The new demotic typography
is **not** a contemporary inven-
tion PAUSE FOR EMPHASIS nor a paradigm shift ,
PAUSE FOR EMPHASIS nor garbage WAIT , CLIFFHANGER
but a return
to a V E R Y old method
of punctuation , NOW EXPLAIN
devised when punctuation served
to indicate the l e n g t h
of pauses , PAUSE ● TO MAKE SURE THEY ABSORB THAT
the **in**tonation and
r^hy_{th}m of phrases
needed
for reading aloud. TA DA

— FRANCES BUTLER

49

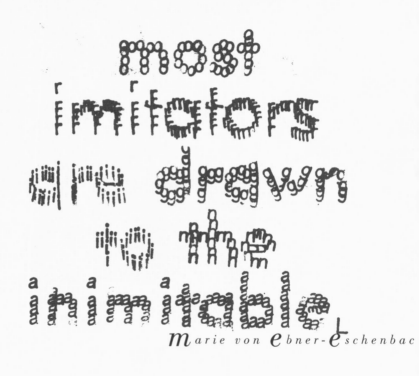

most imitators are drawn to the inimitable

marie von ebner-eschenbac

there are
Kurt Schwitters
numerous typo-
graphic rules.
the most impor-
tant is: do not
ever do it the
way someone
else does.

The design business continues to navel gaze. Designers are still designing for designers rather than working to convince the business world of the importance of design in our everyday lives.
—Joe Duffy

Graphic designers are idea embalmers, loving undertakers preserving bits of data like so many butterflies pinned to felt in a jewel box.
-Paul Saffo

IODIZED SALT

THIS SALT SUPPLIES IODIDE, A NECESSARY NUTRIENT

NET WT. 26 OZ. (1 LB., 10 OZ.) 737 g

53

Just because something
is legible doesn't mean
that it communicates; it
could be communicating
the wrong thing.

DAVID CARSON

My aim is a continuous, sustained, uncontrived image, motivated by nothing but passion.

Rico Lebrun

I wanted to make
orderliness invisible.

I am an anti-grid man.

The best grid is the eye.

When you rely on the eye rather
than on a grid

you're totally

free.

~Leo Lionni

REAL ART HAS THE CAPACITY

TO MAKE US

nervous.

~ susan sontag

Designer seeking ideal type. Please send samples.
I think it is necessary that we should pour the thoughts, which are to be drunk from the book with the eyes, over everything which is perceived by the eyes. The letters and the punctuation marks, which impose order on the thoughts, must be included in our calculations; the way the lines are set out can lead to a particular concentration of thoughts, they must be concentrated for the benefit of the eye too.

—**El Lissitzky**

That's why I think there are two types of people in this world—
people who can start things, and people who can finish things.

And while I place great value on the finishers, its the starters who are rare
because they can envision what isn't there. —Ed Frank

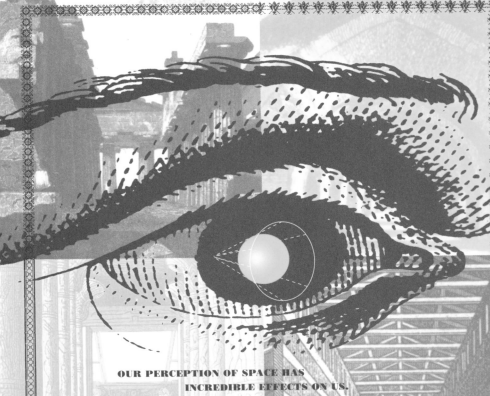

OUR PERCEPTION OF SPACE HAS
INCREDIBLE EFFECTS ON US.
ultimately, it is about our identity:
*who we are and
where we are,*
NOT A MERE FORMAL MATTER.
~ david hockney

Being a good artist means knowing how to think. Good art making is about incorporating your interests It should be about the pursuit of ideas rather than money. Patti Podesta into a whole lifestyle.

FOR ME, DISCOMFORT IS A SIGNAL
OF AN EXCEPTIONAL CONCEPT.

**When I'm totally comfortable with
a concept, I've probably used it before
or seen it somewhere else.**

Discomfort is almost a prerequisite for a great idea.

~ craig frazier

ORIGINAL MIRACLE FORMULA

OVER 25 YEARS OF SUCCESS

The prerequisite of originality is the art of forgetting, at the proper moment, what we know.
-Arthur Koestler

32 FL. OZ. (1 QT.)

You should demand of the writer that he really present what he writes; his ideas reach you through the eye and not through the ear. Therefore typographical form should do by means of optics what the voice and gesture of the writer does to convey his ideas.

el lissitzky

Most people
ignorantly suppose that artists
are the decorators of our human existence,

the esthetes
to whom the cultivated may turn
when the real
business of the day is done....

Far from being **merely decorative,**
the artist's
awareness
is one of the few guardians

of the inherent sanity and equilibrium
of the human spirit
that we have.

— Robert Motherwell

66

worse than becoming
ull the rage. ^{unquote}   rem koolhaas

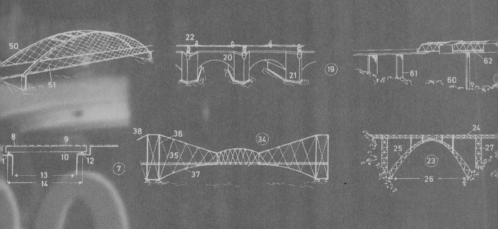

the mere fact that a look has become a style renders it
marginally passé. ^{quote} mike hicks ^{unquote}

67

The grid contains the handwritten answer: **MiltonGlaser**

ACROSS

1 Ground grain
5 Dawn goddess
8 Vatican VIP
12 Recorded proceedings
13 Name in Myanmar's history
14 Ellipse
15 Hotel booking
16 Rash
18 Problems are my friends
20 Munsters' car
21 — Nui (Easter Island)
23 Picnic intruder
24 Intrepid
28 Limp-watch painter
31 Jungfrau, e.g.
32 Mexican food
34 Tease
35 Kennel comments
37 Anonymous
39 Journey segment
41 Indiana city
42 Sharp
45 Porter
49 Vain
51 Bound along
52 Not "fer"
53 Expert
54 PC operator
55 Gadgets for Tiger Woods
56 Orchestra's place
57 Long skirt

DOWN

1 Paddock parent
2 Greenpeace subj.
3 On
4 Delilah, on screen
5 From the Continent
6 Indivisible
7 Similar thing
8 Walesa's territory
9 Go beyond
10 "Annie Oakley"
11 Differently
17 One of the Maunas
19 Cellar contents
22 Music org.
24 "Wings" role
25 Ivy Leaguer
26 Dessert option
27 County of England
29 Fleur-de —
30 Proofs of age

Solution time: 26 min.

7-1

I don't think that all people read in the same way. Today, entire generations are growing up watching MTV and playing video games and it is safe to assume that these people have a high degree of visual sophistication and are not easily discouraged by a lens straightforward or ambiguous typography. On the contrary, they are attracted and enticed to read something because of the visual richness.

RUDY VANDERLANS

IT ISN'T A
QUESTION O
ENHANCEMENT
THROUGH DESIGN
WHETHER A
EDITOR REALIZE
IT OR NOT, DESIGN
IS PART OF WHA
HE DOES EVER
TIME HE PRINT
THE PAPER. -
LOUIS SILVERSTEI

FOR THE LAST DECADE, AS A PROFESSION, GRAPHIC DESIGNERS HAVE BEEN EITHER

shamefully remiss or ineffective about plying their craft for social or political betterment.

–Steven Heller

For the last decade, as a profession, graphic designers have been either shamefully remiss or ineffective about plying their craft for social or political betterment. –Steven Heller

For the last decade, as a profession, graphic designers have been either shamefully remiss or ineffective about plying their craft for social or political betterment. –Steven Heller. For the last decade, as a profession, graphic designers have been either shamefully remiss or ineffective about plying their craft for social or political betterment. –Steven Heller For the last decade, as a profession, graphic designers have been either shamefully remiss or ineffective about plying their craft for social or political betterment.

Anyone who would
letterspace lower case
would steal sheep.

FREDERIC GOUDY

when you are having trouble defining something it is often easier to define what it
is NOT, and the vernacular is what we [profes-
sional graphic designers] are not.

— jeffrey keedy

I find going to bed and pulling my imagination over my head often means waking up with a solution to a design problem. That state of limbo, the time between sleeping and waking, seems to allow ideas to somehow outflank the sentinels of common sense. That's when they can float to the surface. I find ideas often show up in the shower, or while I'm contemplating marmalade and toast at breakfast.

Alan Fletcher

You
should
never
lose
sight
of the
fact
that
you
are
solving
somebody's
problems.
At the
same
time,
you
should
solve
your
own
as well.

Lucille Tenazas

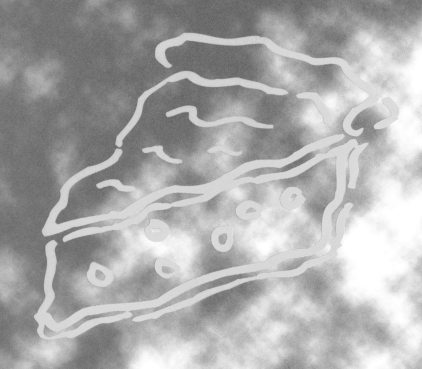

It's not rocket science. It's social science—the science of understanding people's needs and their unique relationship with art, literature, history, music, work, philosophy, community, technology and psychology. The act of design is structuring and creating that balance.

~ Clement Mok

I've always considered myself a graphic artist—a draftsman—as opposed to being a typist. I do still work on a drawing table. At times drawing on a computer feels like I'm drawing on an Etch-a-Sketch.

—Michael Schwab

Computer design...

is quite often merely bad design

done on a computer.

—MIKE HICKS

Color is a creative element, not a trimming.

—Piet Zwart

The works must be conceived with fire in the soul

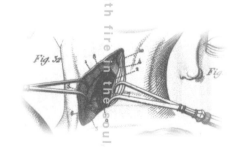

Fig. 52

Fig

ut executed with clinical coolness

—Joan Miró

Your mind is like a tipi. Leave the entrance flap open so that the fresh air can enter and clear out the

SMOKE

OF CONFUSION

— CHIEF EAGLE, TETON SIOUX

When I design, I don't consider the technical or commercial parameters so much as the desire for a dream that humans have attempted to project onto an object. —Philippe Starck

**Computers are worthless.
They can only give you answers.**
—Pablo Picasso

`OK`

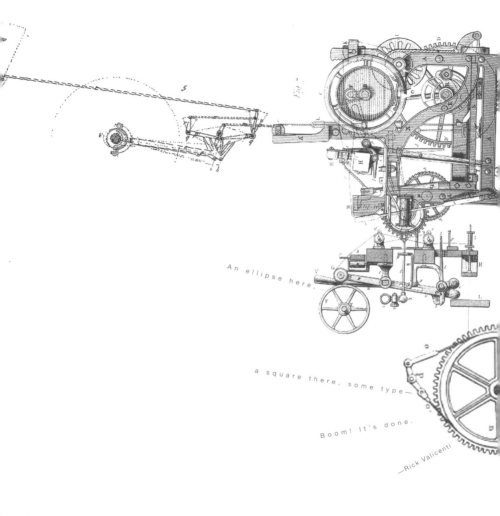

An ellipse here,

a square there, some type—

Boom! It's done.

—Rick Valicenti

**The challenge
is for the graphic
designer to turn
data into information
and information
into messages
of meaning.**
-Katherine McCoy

NET WT. 1 LB. (16 OZ.) 453g

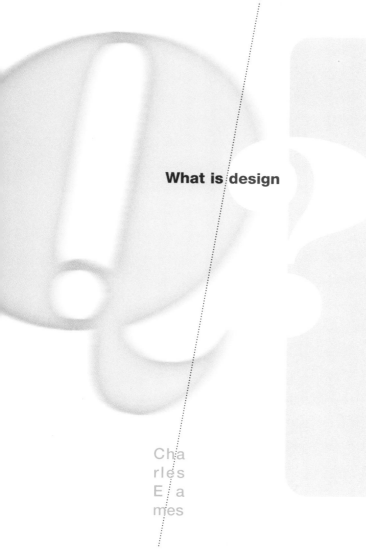

What is design

A plan for arranging elements in such a way as to best accomplish a particular purpose.

Cha
rles
E a
mes

GEOMETRY CAN PRODUCE
LEGIBLE LETTERS, BUT
ART ALONE MAKES THEM
BEAUTIFUL
ART BEGINS WHERE
GEOMETRY ENDS, AND
IMPARTS TO LETTERS A
CHARACTER TRANSCENDING
MERE MEASUREMENT.
paul standard

WE USE THE LETTERS OF OUR ALPHABET EVERY DAY
WITH THE UTMOST EASE AND UNCONCERN, TAKING THEM
ALMOST AS MUCH FOR GRANTED AS THE AIR WE
BREATHE. WE DO NOT REALIZE THAT EACH OF THESE
LETTERS IS AT OUR SERVICE TODAY ONLY AS THE RESULT
OF A LONG AND LABORIOUSLY SLOW PROCESS OF

E V O L U T I O N

IN THE AGE-OLD ART OF WRITING.
d o u g l a s   c .   m c m u r t i e

My errors were more fertile than I ever imagine

Jan Tschichol

Sometimes I'm amazed that I spend my day creating magic and fantasy and that people buy it. It's like connecting with the inner child in me; I'm just having a great time, and I'm chuckling to myself that this is really happening, that I can do this with my life.

–Lita Albuquerque

EVERYTHING IS CONSUMED

BY STYLE AND FASHION,
AND WHEN I SAY FASHION,
I DON'T MEAN CLOTHES,
BUT TASTE, WHICH IS
SOCIALLY CONSTRUCTED
AND GRANTS POWER
AND TAKES IT AWAY.

100% PRESHRUNK COTTON
MADE IN U.S.A.
CARE ON REVERSE
X-LARGE (46 - 48)

BARBARA KRUGER

[Degenerate type is] a form of canned cynicism which will doom its perpetrators to a special room in hell where lovely little children of all races, creeds, and religions are eternally bathed in gentle rosy and amber glows, singing "It's a Small World After All." There's no legitimate typographic reason to create an alphabet which looks like it leaked out of a diaper.

PETER FRATERDEUS

Urban public space is a stage for viewing the field of graphic design in its diversity.

diversity.

A mix of voices, *from advertising to activism,* compete for visibility

FOOD CASH & CARF

OPEN TO PUBLIC

COMPANION®

AUTHENTIC SINCE 1958

良友牌

北加州特約経銷產

大三元
100

泰國 米王牌香米

米王牌香米

本公司併售
祖庙牌草菇老抽,老抽王,生抽王 登重
絵銷批賣

4
0
1

—ELLEN LUPTON

BOX TOPS

These days, information is a commodity being sold. And designers–including the newly defined subset of information designers and information architects– have a responsible role to play. We are interpreters-not merely translators- between sender and receiver. What we say and how we say it makes a differ- ence. If we want to speak to people, we need to know their language. In order to design for understanding, we need to understand design. -Erik Spiekermann

NET WT. 17 OZ.
(1LB. 1 OZ.)(482 GRAMS)

GRAPHIC WILL SAVE TI

RIGHT
DOES

Develop an infallible
technique and then place

yourself

at the mercy of inspiration.

ZEN MAXIM

DESIGN
E WORLD
FTER ROCK & ROLL

DAVID CARSON

A good SOLUTION,

in addition to being

RIGHT, should have

PERMANENCE IS UP TO GOD.

the potential for

LONGEVITY. Yet I don't

think one can design

for PERMANENCE. One

designs for FUNCTION,

for USEFULNESS,

RIGHTNESS, BEAUTY.

Permanence is up to

God.

PAUL RAND

Client wants:

① GOOD

② FAST

③ CHEAP

Designer replies: PICK TWO

TAKE-OUT TAX   .08
TOTAL   1.07
CASH TEND   5.00
CHANGE   3.93

PHOTOGRAPHY BY MICHELLE L. BENZER

—Advice from Hugh Dubberly

I DO THINK THERE IS SOMETHING TO

BE SAID FOR ART WHICH IS JUST SORT OF

LUKEWARM...THE KINDS OF THINGS

THAT I'M ATTRACTED TO ARE NONCHALANT.

—EDWARD GOREY

One of the
tragedies of
the design
scene is
that it always
acts

—Hans-Rudolf Lutz

too late.

Right now it's only

a notion,

but I think I could get money

to turn it into

a concept

and then later

develop it into

an idea.

—from *Annie Hall*

are any ideas really new?

-marty neumeier

sources

Every effort has been made to track down sources for the quotes included in this book. If something has been overlooked, please alert the publisher.

Lita Albuquerque. *Art Work: Choosing a Life in Art*, ed. Karen Jacobson, interviews and text by Laurence Drieband and Wendy Adest. Pasadena: Art Center College of Design, 1994. p. 91.

Andy Altmann. *Designers on Mac*, text by Diane Burns. Tokyo; Graphic-sha, 1992. p. 39.

From **Annie Hall. Four Films by Woody Allen.** New York: Random House, 1982. p. 102.

Francis Bacon. *Francis Bacon: In Conversation with Michel Archimbaud.* London: Phaidon Press Ltd., 1993. p. 9.

Hugo Ball. "Return of the Son of the Author as Typographer: Literary Parlor Games" by Alastair Johnston. *The Ampersand*, vol. 11, no. 4, Winter 1992. p. 26.

Saul Bass. Source unknown. p. 44.

Georges Braque. *Francis Bacon: In Conversation with Michel Archimbaud.* p. 8.

Neville Brody. "Neville Brody" by Rick Poynor. *Eye* magazine, vol. 2, no. 6, 1992. Reprinted by permission of *Eye.* p. 42.

Aaron Burns. *Graphic Design in America: A Visual Language History*, ed. Mildred Friedman, et al. Minneapolis: Walker Art Center/New York: Harry N. Abrams, Inc., 1989. p. 12.

Frances Butler. "New Demotics and the Nostalgic Dreamland" by Frances Butler. *AIGA Journal of Graphic Design*, vol. 12, no. 2, 1994. p. 49.

David Carson. *The End of Print: The Graphic Design of David Carson* by Lewis Blackwell and David Carson. San Francisco: Chronicle Books, 1995. p. 54.

David Carson. *The End of Print: The Graphic Design of David Carson.* p. 96-7.

Ivan Chermayeff. *Graphic Design in America: A Visual Language History.* p. 22.

Ivan Chermayeff. "The Designer as Ventriloquist" by Ivan Chermayeff. *AIGA Journal of Graphic Design*, vol. 12, no. 2, 1994. p. 4.

Chief Eagle. "Talk of Design: Prisoners of the Image" by Michael Gray. *AIGA Journal of Graphic Design*, vol. 12, no. 2, 1994. p. 82.

Fyodor Dostoyevsky. *The Idiot* by Fyodor Dostoyevsky. New York: New American Library, 1969. p. 45.

Joe Duffy. "*How* Top 10" by Rick Tharp. *How* magazine, January 1996. p. 52.

Hugh Dubberly. Spring portfolio course, San Jose State University, 1993. p. 99.

William Addison Dwiggins. *Stop Stealing Sheep and Find Out How Type Works* by Erik Spiekermann and E. M. Ginger. Mountain View: Adobe Press, 1993. p. 38.

Charles Eames. Source unknown. p. 87.

Marie von Ebner-Eschenbach. *Branding with Type* by Stefan Rögener, Albert-Jan Pool, and Ursula Packhäuser, ed. by E. M. Ginger. Mountain View: Adobe Press, 1995. p. 50.

Alan Fletcher. "Secrets of Design: Rebellion" by Marty Neumeier. *Critique* magazine, Autumn 1996. Reprinted by permission of *Critique*. p. 74.

Alan Fletcher. Source unknown. p. 19.

Adrian Forty. Source unknown. p. 36–7.

Ed Frank. "Code Warrior" by Tom Abate. *San Francisco Examiner* Magazine, December 8, 1996. p. 59.

Peter Fraterdeus. "Rumors of the Death of Typography Have Been Greatly Exaggerated" by Peter Fraterdeus. *AIGA Journal of Graphic Design*, vol. 14, no. 3. Reprinted by permission of Peter Fraterdeus. p. 93.

Craig Frazier. "Secrets of Design: Rebellion." p. 62.

Emmanuel Geibel. *Manuale Typographicum* by Hermann Zapf. Originally reprinted in *Gesammelte Werke*, vol. 2. Stuttgart, 1883. p. 43.

Milton Glaser. Source unknown. p. 68.

Milton Glaser. *Graphic Design in America: A Visual Language History.* p. 48.

Johann Wolfgang von Goethe. *Branding with Type.* p. 34.

Edward Gorey. *The World of Edward Gorey* by Clifford Ross and Karen Wilkin. New York: Harry N. Abrams, Inc., 1996. p. 100.

Frederic Goudy. *Stop Stealing Sheep and Find Out How Type Works.* p. 72.

April Greiman. *Hybrid Imagery: April Greiman.* New York: Watson-Guptill Publications, 1990. p. 31.

April Greiman. *Graphic Design in America: A Visual Language History.* p. 25.

Steven Heller. "Guerrilla Graphics" by Steven Heller. *Looking Closer: Critical Writings on Graphic Design*, eds. Michael Bierut, William Drenttel, Steven Heller, and D.K. Holland. New York: Allsworth Press, 1994. Originally reprinted in *Eye*, vol. 1, no.4, 1991. p. 71.

Robert Henri. *The Art Spirit*, compiled by Margery A. Ryerson. Philadelphia/New York: J. B. Lippincott Company, 1960. p. 17.

Mike Hicks. "The Rise and Curdling of Modernism" by Mike Hicks. *Graphis* magazine, vol. 51, May/June 1995. p. 67.

Mike Hicks. "The Rise and Curdling of Modernism." p. 79.

David Hockney. *That's the Way I See It* by David Hockney, ed. Nikos Stangos. San Francisco: Chronicle Books, 1993. p. 60.

Eiko Ishioka. "Bridging Design with Art" by Paolo Polledri. *Graphis* magazine, vol. 51, May/June 1995. p. 27.

Karrie Jacobs. *Looking Closer: Critical Writings on Graphic Design.* p. 76.

James Jebbia. "Cease and Desist: Issues of Cultural Reappropriation in Urban Street Design" by Kevin Lyons. *AIGA Journal of Graphic Design*, vol. 14, no. 1, 1996. p. 40.

Tibor Kalman. "5 Top Designers Confess: I Never Went to Art School" by Philip Meggs. *Print* magazine, May/June 1996. p. 47.

Jeffery Keedy. *Lift and Separate: Graphic Design and the Quote Vernacular Unquote* ed. by Barbara Glauber. New York: Cooper Union for the Advancement of Science and Art, 1993. p. 73.

Arthur Koestler. "Zigzag Thinking" by Roy R. Behrens. *AIGA Journal of Graphic Design*, vol. 12, no. 4, 1995. p. 63.

Rem Koolhaas. Source unknown. p. 66–7.

Barbara Kruger. *Art Work: Choosing a Life in Art.* p. 92.

Rico Lebrun. *Conversations with Artists* by Selden Rodman. New York: Capricorn Books, 1961. p. 55.

Zuzana Licko. *Emigre: Graphic Design into the Digital Realm* by Rudy VanderLans and Zuzana Licko with Mary E. Gray. New York: Byron Preiss/Van Nostrand Reinhold, 1993. p. 41.

Leo Lionni. *Graphic Design in America: A Visual Language History.* p. 56.

El Lissitzky. *El Lissitzky: Life, Letters, Texts* by Sophie Lissitzky-Küppers. Greenwich, Connecticut: New York Graphic Society Ltd./London: Thames and Hudson Ltd., 1968. p. 58.

El Lissitzky. *El Lissitzky: Life, Letters, Texts.* p. 64.

Raymond Loewy. *Terence Conran on Design* by Terence Conran. Woodstock: The Overlook Press, 1996. p. 32.

Ellen Lupton. *Mixing Messages: Graphic Design in Contemporary Culture* by Ellen Lupton. New York: Cooper-Hewitt National Design Museum, Smithsonian Institution, and Princeton Architectural Press, 1996. p. 94.

Alvin Lustig. Source unknown. p. 18.

Alvin Lustig. *The Collected Writings of Alvin Lustig* ed. by Holland R. Melson, Jr. New Haven, Conn: H. R. Melson, Jr., 1958. p. 28.

Hans-Rudolf Lutz. "Hans-Rudolf Lutz" by Yvonne Schwemer-Scheddin. *Eye* magazine, vol. 6, no. 23, Winter 1996. p. 101.

Michael Mabry. "Michael Mabry" by Ken Coupland. *Graphis* magazine, November/December 1994. p. 35.

Kasimir Malevich. *Autocritique: Essays on Art and Anti-Art, 1963-1987* by Barbara Rose. New York: Weidenfeld & Nicolson, 1988. Originally reprinted in *Suprematism* by Kasimir Malevich, 1919. p. 7.

Glenn Martinez. *"How* Top 10" by Rick Tharp, *How* magazine, January 1996. p. 16.

Katherine McCoy. *Women in Design: A Contemporary View* by Liz McQuiston. New York: Rizzoli, 1988. p. 86.

Douglas C. McMurtrie. *Manuale Typographicum* by Hermann Zapf. Originally printed in *The Book: The Story of Printing and Bookmaking* by Douglas C. McMurtrie. New York/London/Toronto: Marboro Books, 1950. p. 89.

Duane Michals. *Art Work: Choosing a Life in Art.* p. 6.

Joan Miró. *Joaquim Gomis. Joan Miró: Photographs 1941-1981*, text by Daniel Giralt-Miracle. Barcelona: Editorial Gustavo Gili, S.A., 1994. p. 81.

Clement Mok. AIGA Information Graphics: Design of Understanding 2 exhibition entry form. Reprinted by permission of Clement Mok. p. 77.

Robert Motherwell. *From Lascaux to Brooklyn* by Paul Rand. New Haven/London: Yale University Press, 1996. p. 65.

Hideki Nakajima. "Illustration Today: A Global Forum" by Stuart Frolick. *Graphis* magazine, vol. 52, July/August 1996. p. 15.

George Nelson. Source unknown. p. 30.

Marty Neumeier. "Welcome" by Marty Neumeier, paraphrasing Gene Fowler. *Critique* magazine, Autumn 1996. p. 11.

Marty Neumeier. "Welcome" by Marty Neumeier. *Critique* magazine, Autumn 1996. p. 103.

David Ogilvy. *Typography 16: The Annual of the Type Directors Club, 41st Exhibition.* New York: Watson-Guptill Publications, 1995. Originally reprinted in *I Can't Read This: And I Designed It*, ed. Michael Skjei. Minneapolis, Minnesota: Shay, Shea, Hsieh, and Skjei, Publishers, 1994. p. 33.

Georgia O'Keeffe. Spoken by the author in 1976. Reprinted in *The New Beacon Book of Quotations by Women* by Rosalie Maggio. Boston: Beacon Press, 1996. p. 14.

Pablo Picasso. "Secrets of Design: Rebellion." p. 84.

Patti Podesta. *Art Work: Choosing a Life in Art.* p. 61.

Paul Rand. *Graphic Design in America: A Visual Language History.* p. 98

Paul Rand. Source unknown. p. 46.

Wendy Richmond. "Using Your Imagination" by Wendy Richmond. *Communication Arts* magazine, vol. 37, no. 3, July 1995. p. 13.

Paul Saffo. "The Electric Piñata" by Paul Saffo. *I.D.* magazine, vol. 42, no. 1, January/February 1995. p. 53.

Antoine de Saint Exupéry. *The Little Prince* by Antoine de Saint-Exupéry. San Diego: Harcourt Brace Javoanovich, 1982. p. 24.

George Santayana. *AIGA Journal of Graphic Design*, vol. 12, no. 4, 1995. p. 29.

Michael Schwab. "Beauty of the Brush and Page" by Merrill C. Berman and Denise Urell. *Graphis* magazine, vol. 52, no. 304, July/August 1996. p. 78.

Kurt Schwitters. *Branding with Type.* p. 51.

Leslie Sherr. "Starck Transformation" by Leslie Sherr. *u&lc: Upper and Lower Case*, vol. 23, no. 3, Winter 1996. p. 23.

Louis Silverstein. *Graphic Design in America: A Visual Language History.* p. 70.

Susan Sontag. *The New Beacon Book of Quotations by Women.* p. 57.

Erik Spiekermann. AIGA Information Graphics: Design for Understanding 2 exhibition entry form. Reprinted by permission of Erik Spiekermann. p. 95.

Paul Standard. *Manuale Typographicum* by Hermann Zapf. p. 88.

Philippe Starck. "Starck Transformation." p. 83.

Lucille Tenazas. Source unknown. p. 75.

Oliviero Toscani. "Oliviero Toscani: Communications Maveric" by Mike Hicks. *Graphis* magazine, May/June 1994. p. 36–7.

Henri-Marie-Raymond de Toulouse-Lautrec. Source unknown. p. 5.

Jan Tschichold. Source unknown. p. 90.

Rick Valicenti. Source unknown. p. 85.

Rudy VanderLans. *Emigre: Graphic Design into the Digital Realm.* Reprinted by permission of *Emigre*. p. 69.

Massimo Vignelli. Source unknown. p. 3.

Diana Vreeland. *Terence Conran on Design.* p. 20.

Lorraine Wild. "Grading Education: The ID Debate" by Chea Pearlman. *I.D.* magazine, September/October 1991. p. 21.

Fred Woodward. "Woodward Rocks On" by Peter Hall. *u&lc: Upper and Lower Case*, vol. 23, no. 3, Winter 1996. p. 10.

Zen maxim. *Conversations with Artists.* p. 96.

Piet Zwart. Source unknown. p. 80.